To

Dad (Grandad)

Happy ~~Birthday~~ Fathers day 2003.

Lots of love

always

Nick, Sarah, Kerry

Emily + Tom Tom.

X X X X X

My Memories of
SPURS
By Bobby Smith
A Britespot Publication

FOREWORD

Jimmy Greaves

Bobby Smith is universally remembered as one of the greatest strikers of his generation – a strong, bustling, classic type of centre forward who was utterly fearless in front of defenders and goalposts alike.

That's not a bad way to be remembered, but Bobby was much more than that. I've lost count of the number of games we played together for Spurs and England but I can assure you that over the years he created a lot more chances for me than I did for him.

His strength and commitment often detracted from the fact that he was actually very handy with his head and his feet and a fantastic player to have partnering you up front.

Luckily for Bobby his place in footballing history is assured. Not only is he still Spurs' second highest ever aggregate goal scorer with 208 goals in 317 games but his tally of 33 during the 1961 Double Winning season means his name will be revered as long as football is played at White Hart Lane.

His England record isn't too bad either. In the 15 games he played for his country he scored 13 goals, including one against Northern Ireland on his debut, and I can't think of any other striker before or since who has netted close to a goal a game in international football.

Although he scared a lot of people on the pitch everyone loved him off it. We've been good friends for over forty years now and I can honestly say that as long as there's not a football about he's one of life's true gentlemen!

Left: England's Bobby Smith (c) is thwarted by Rest of the World's Svatopluk Pluskal (l) and Milutin Soskic (r)

My Memories of Spurs by Bobby Smith
A Britespot Publication

First Published in Great Britain by
Britespot Publishing Solutions Limited
Chester Road, Cradley Heath, West Midlands B64 6AB

© Britespot December 2002

ISBN 1 904103 08 1

Cover design and layout
© Britespot Publishing Solutions Limited

Printed and bound in Great Britain by:
The Cromwell Press,
Aintree Avenue,
White Horse Business Park,
Trowbridge,
Wiltshire,
BA14 OXB

My thanks to Roger Marshall, Paul Burns, Linda Perkins and Steve Parry of Britespot Publishing for making the publishing of this book possible.

My thanks to Iain McCartney who has helped me put into words all my memories.

Britespot would like to thank James Cadman who has developed the concept of the 'My Memories Books' with the individual players and acting as a contributing author for the series.

Photos: ©Empics, Colorsport and Les Gold Promotions.

CONTENTS

Chapters

Page

My Memories Of

SPURS By Bobby Smith

Left: Bobby and his Wife Jean

Chapter 1

FROM TEESIDE TO TOTTENHAM
At the Beginning

Although I played all of my senior football in London and the south of England, it might come as surprise to many, to discover that I was in fact from the North-East.

I was born on February 22nd 1933, in Scarth Street, Lingdale, a small mining village near Middlesbrough, which wasn't such a nondescript place as it sounds, as former 'Boro hero George Hardwick spent his early years in the same environs.

My playing career began, like almost all other professionals, with the local schools side, Lingdale Council School, before joining Redcar United and then Redcar Boys Club. I also had a short spell with nursery side of Chelsea Football Club, who went by the quaint name of Tudor Rose.

Playing for Redcar Boys, was a far cry from what I was to become used to in later years, as our 'home' ground was basically a piece of waste land behind the Redcar racecourse. I still recall how primitive it really was. No changing rooms, nothing.

We would change in the open air, leave our clothes, under the watchful eye of one of our friends, alongside one of the touchlines. If it rained, we would cover them with someone's raincoat or whatever.

In those days, because I was a well-built youngster, I played mainly as a defender, a full back. But, as has happened to numerous other players over the years, I found myself in a new position one Saturday when a team- mate failed to show up. The missing individual was our centre forward. I was now expected to score goals rather than prevent them.

To say I enjoyed the experience is something of an understatement. Scoring four goals perhaps having something to do with it.

In any case, Redcar had found a new centre forward and I had found the position that was going to take me into the world of professional football.

The complete transformation to centre forward did not come immediately, as I still found myself selected from, time to time, in my old position of full back, but my clean break from my defensive duties came in a cup tie against South Bank Juniors. Our usual centre forward failed to turn up and the rest of the team were rather reluctant when asked to play at centre forward. In the end, I stepped forward and said that I would give it a go.

FROM TEESIDE TO TOTTENHAM

Unfortunately, we lost 3-2, but I scored our two goals and found my true position.

However, everyone needs a lucky break in life and I got mine when Redcar Boy's Club reached a local Cup Final.

For one reason or another, with the kick off drawing near, our centre forward had failed to show and yours truly was once again asked to fill the breech.

I was really up for the Final anyway, but being pushed into the forward line gave me that extra buzz and I went out and scored six times in our 7-1 win, as we lifted the trophy.

Unknown to me, one of the spectators scattered around the pitch was Tommy Robinson, a scout for Chelsea and at the final whistle, as I made my way from the pitch, the chap who ran our club caught up with me and enthusiastically exclaimed that Chelsea had been watching me. "Their scout was impressed by your performance" he went on, "and he wants to have a talk with you at home".

What better news could a fourteen year old, football mad youngster want?
I often thought though, that if we had been faced with stronger opposition that afternoon, who had a better defence, I might have had fewer scoring chances and my future would have been entirely different.

Anyway, arrangements were made for Tommy Robinson to visit my parents a couple of days later and I seemed to spend night and day thinking of little else.

Thankfully the meeting went well and I was invited down to London for a fortnight's trial, with my parents quite happy to give me their backing to a career in professional football.

However, like George Best upon his arrival in Manchester from Belfast, I was immediately homesick, overcome by the enormity of everything in London. Not surprising really for a fourteen-year-old from a small, scarcely populated village in the North-East, finding himself alone in the capital. Completely overcome by it all, I returned home after a matter of days.

Chelsea, much to my later relief, were not simply content to let me return home to rejoin Redcar and forget about me. Contacting my father, they asked if he would like to come down to London with me. That was if I wanted to return.

FROM TEESIDE TO TOTTENHAM

Personally, I was a bit apprehensive about making the return journey, but my father more or less made up my mind for me, agreeing to spend two weeks with me in London, helping me to settle in.

My father's reassurance helped me tremendously and after staying with an aunt, who lived not far from Chelsea's Stamford Bridge ground in Sloane Square, I moved into club digs with some other apprentices, having signed amateur forms in May 1947.

Following my initial failure to settle in, I soon adapted to city life and was rewarded for my endurance and hard work, with a place in the Chelsea junior side.

One of the early matches that I can remember was another Cup Final (you never forget the big ones), in the London Minor Cup, surprisingly enough against Tottenham Hotspur's juniors at Stamford Bridge.

The Spurs team was made of a bit sterner stuff than the opposition that I faced in my last Cup Final appearance and there was no repeat 7-1 scoreline. Chelsea, however, did run out winners, by 3-0 and I did my career prospects no harm whatsoever by scoring all three.

The opposing centre half that day, whom I got the better of was later to become a good friend and also a team mate after I joined Tottenham. His name was Tony Marchi.

Under the guidance of Albert Tennat and Dick Foss, at Chelsea, my game began to develop and I was soon to experience European football for the first time, as we went on a two week tour of Denmark. My early European adventures were later to continue with England youth, playing against Switzerland Youth in Vienna. It was all a bit strange to me being away from home, but I enjoyed the experience of that trip to Denmark and I think we won two of our four games, drawing the other two.

Progress through the ranks at Stamford Bridge was steady, if not spectacular and I obtained my fair share of goals. I even found myself playing inside forward for a time, a position I was also to fill in my early days at White Hart Lane.

It was, however, in the centre forward position that that I made my Chelsea League debut, against Bolton Wanders at Burnden Park in September 1950.

Chelsea
Football Club
Season 1951-2

Football League—Division I

CHELSEA
v.
BURNLEY

Saturday, 19th April, 1952

Kick-off 3 p.m.

OFFICIAL PROGRAMME

6d

STAMFORD BRIDGE GROUNDS LONDON SW6
THE RIGHT OF ADMISSION TO GROUNDS IS RESERVED

The early season fixture was played on a Monday night, yes we did play at such times back then, but there was certainly no Sky TV there to record my introduction into League football and catalogue away for posterity. The only people who were to witness the momentous occasion, for me anyway, were those who paid their money at the turnstiles.

The match wouldn't have made riveting viewing in any case, as it was not a particularly good game, with Chelsea losing 1-0.

Prior to kick off, the Bolton centre forward, Nat Lofthouse wished me well, which I thought was a nice sporting gesture, coming from a more experienced professional.

My head to head opponent that night was another familiar name – Matt Gillies, who went on to play and manage Leicester City.

At Stamford Bridge with Chelsea, I scored thirty goals in eighty-six senior appearances, not a bad average, but three goals in an F.A. Cup tie against Leeds United in 1951-52 are perhaps more fondly remembered than some of the others.

The match in question was played at Villa Park, as it was I think a fifth round second replay and it brought me face to face with a man who is today a footballing legend, John Charles.

Although I was still only nineteen and learning, I some how got the better of the big Welshman on that occasion.

My departure from the 'Pensioners' was totally unexpected and at first not something I even considered at first, despite finding myself in and out of the first team.

I was training at Stamford Bridge one cold December morning in 1955, when the secretary's assistant suddenly appeared and informed me that the manager, Ted Drake, wanted to see me in his office right away. I had no idea what it could be about, so I was certainly puzzled as I made my way there.
Arriving at his office, I was even more surprised to find not only Ted Drake there but also Jimmy Anderson, the Tottenham Hotspur manager and his assistant Bill Nicholson.

Getting straight to the point, Ted Drake informed me that Tottenham had made an offer of £17,000 for my services and that Chelsea had accepted it.

My Memories Of

SHOW THEM

By CLIVE TOYE

BOBBY SMITH, the man who put
"heart" in White Hart-lane, scor...
...als which beat Burnley in a mood o...
...ry after lashing the men who have m...
...e through Soccer hell.

The hell: The nagging nerves from the ...
...nich took him to the brink of the drop ...
...purs and England teams.

The torturers: The critics and the fans who
...epeatedly insisted: "Smith must go."
And the bitter attack from the normally imperturbable
...'t mind being told I'm not good enough for
...opinions.

SPURS SIGN BO...
...ham attacks.

They play him against Luton

Evening Standard Football Reporter HAROLD PALMER

Spurs have got Bobby Smith after all. The Chelsca
centre-forward who recently refused to agree to be
transferred to the Tottenham club changed his mind
and signed for Spurs today.

He will be in the Tottenham
League side for the Saturday
morning game with Luton
Town at White Hart Lane.

Spurs have paid £20,000 for
this strong, bustling forward
whose transfer they have
sought for some time.

"Spurs have never let us alone,
and I don't blame them," said
Chelsea manager Ted Drake.
"Bob' did not like leaving us
but he has not had a lot of chance
here, and he realised he had a
chance to establish himself at
Tottenham."

Tottenham manager Jimmy
Anderson was jubilant. "I have
been very sweet on Smith ever
since he played for Chelsea Juniors,
before he signed professional. We
have the footballers here. I think
Smith's spirit will finish it off for
us."

Smith, who joined ...
Juniors from Redcar in ...
born near Middles...
signed as a profes...
sea in May 1950 ...
his position ...

Smith ...
with ...
Chel...
h...

E MAGIC EYE
NAPS SMITH

HAYWARD

...MITH

...MITH A MIGHTY M...

...TWO GOALS INCREASE SPURS' LEAD

...NG

...ys the ref. But Smith has his revenge w...

FROM TEESIDE TO TOTTENHAM

To say that I was surprised is an understatement, but the tables were soon turned, when I politely informed them that I was happy at Chelsea and did not want to leave. Tottenham, I might add, were at that time languishing near the bottom of the first Division and could be considered inferior to Chelsea.

Anyway, I left the three open mouthed figures in the office underneath the main stand and made my way back onto the pitch to continue training.

One of my best friends at the club, my mentor if you like, was captain, Roy Bentley and he quickly made a bee- line for me to inquire about my sudden summons.

I told him of Tottenham's approach and how I had turned it down point blank. Roy, took me aback a little, when he said that it would be "a big mistake" on my behalf to turn down the opportunity of joining a club, who despite their lowly position did have the potential to improve. He also made it quite clear that there would be little or no future for me at Chelsea, as they had accepted the offer and were obviously prepared to let me go and that I had had one or two confrontations with Ted Drake in the past, with this latest episode liable to make things a bit more strained between us.

Quickly reassessing the situation, with Roy prompting that I should "run back and agree to join them", as it was something that he would certainly do, given the opportunity. I made my way back into the bowels of the stand to the manager's office.

Knocking on the door and answering the "come in", I entered the office to find only Ted Drake sat behind his desk. "Yes?" he gruffly asked.

Upon telling him that I had changed my mind, He replied that the Spurs contingent had just left.

In desperation, I turned and ran in the direction of the car park, arriving there just as their car was pulling away.

Surprised by my sudden appearance, Jimmy Anderson slowed his car to a halt and rolled down the window. I breathlessly explained that I had had second thoughts and if they still wanted me, I would be happy to join Tottenham.

His delight was obvious and to my surprise, he removed his wallet from his jacket pocket and handed me a crisp ten pound note. That was my signing on fee. I was now, more or less, a Tottenham Hotspur player.

Playing at Blackburn, August 1960. Norman heads clear from Dougan.

Chapter 2

TOTTENHAM
The Early Days and my New Team Mates

Only four years had passed since Tottenham had won the Football League Championship, but they were now struggling to try and recapture the form of that period, when the likes of Ramsey, Nicholson, Burgess, Baily and Ditchburn ruled the roost. That particular team, however, was beginning to age and one of manager Jimmy Anderson's reasons for signing me was to replace another of the stars of that time, Len Duquemin.

I fitted into the way of things at White Hart Lane without much of a problem, playing most of my games at inside forward, actually partnering the man I was to eventually replace. In the remainder of that first season, I managed to score thirteen goals in twenty-seven League and Cup appearances.

Over the next few years, we slowly gelled together, but it wasn't until Bill Nicholson took over the manager's role from Jimmy Anderson in October 1958, that the signs of progress began to come a little more distinct.

Already at the club prior to the change in managers was the nucleus of what was to become a memorable side. A team that was to re-write the history books of not only Tottenham Hotspur, but of British football in general.

Danny Blanchflower had joined Tottenham from Aston Villa in December 1954 for somewhere in the region of £30,000, having previously played for Glentoran and Barnsley. He was also a Northern Ireland internationalist.

Two years prior to Blanchflower's arrival, full back Peter Baker had signed professional, stepping up from non-League football. Like myself, Peter was seen as a replacement for one of the 1951-52 Championship side and took over from Alf Ramsey. Ramsey himself, going onto a highly successful career in management at both league and international level.

Outside left Terry Dyson and another full back, Ron Henry had both been at the club for a year when I arrived. The diminutive five foot three inch Dyson, a Yorkshire man, had initially been signed as an amateur in December 1954, whilst on National Service. Despite his lack of inches, he was soon to become a handful for numerous full backs.

Ron Henry was a team mate of Terry's in the Army side and was also signed as an amateur at first.

One month previous to my joining Tottenham, centre half Maurice Norman was signed from Norwich City. Initially, he was a full back, but switched to centre half the following year.

It wasn't, as I said, until after our change in manager that things began to look up, as Bill Nicholson realised that if Tottenham were going to achieve any of their former glory, then improvements had to be made. In less than two years, he had assembled a team who were to become one of the top teams in the country.

The first player to arrive as Bill's team building got under way, was outside right Cliff Jones, in Feb 1959.

Cliff, I recall, came from a footballing family and cost £35,000 when signed from Swansea. He was a very intelligent player and someone to whom I was frequently grateful for supplying me with numerous goalscoring opportunities.

Next, came a player who makes today's so called 'hardmen' look like soft touches. A player who added the grit to our midfield, Dave Mackay.

A £30,000 buy from Hearts, Dave was a dynamic personality and his strength and determination won us many games.

The final three pieces of Bill Nicholson's jigsaw arrived prior to the start of that season and in the early months of that particular campaign.

The first to arrive was goalkeeper Bill Brown from Dundee, a replacement for a Tottenham legend, Ted Ditchburn.

Next came another Scot, a player admired by team mates and opponents alike, John White. The 'Ghost' as he was called, for his ability to simply appear from nowhere, came from Falkirk for £20,000 and was an immensely skilful inside forward, who could create a goal out of nothing.

Last, but not least, was Les Allen, who came from my old club Chelsea, in a straight swap for Johnny Brooks.

It took Les a while to win over our sometimes fickle supporters, but a five goal performance in a record breaking 13-2 F.A. Cup replay win against Crewe at White Hart Lane, two months after his arrival, won them over.

So there we have it. A team for all seasons and a team who were soon to become household names in the very near future.

Despite the team having something of a new look to it in the latter half of season 1959-60, we were one of the teams involved in the Championship race, whilst also harbouring hopes of a favourable Cup run following our 13-2 4th round trouncing of Crewe Alexandra.

Sadly, our Cup dreams came to an end in the following round, when Blackburn Rovers produced a surprising 3-1 victory at White Hart Lane.

On the League front, once the dreams of a League and Cup double had been extinguished, we had Wolves and Burnley as our main challengers, if that is the correct term to use, as we only realistically had an outside chance of lifting the title. As things were to turn out, we did have a big say in its eventual destination.

A trip to favourites Wolves towards the end of April was crucial to the final outcome, for despite Burnley's games in hand it would have more or less given the Midlands side the trophy. However, as it turned out, we won 3-1 and taking some inspiration from that result, Burnley sneaked up on the outside to take the Championship. We finished third, two points behind.

Despite our obvious disappointment, our target was set.

'Spurs' 1959-60

John Brooks

Chapter 3

MEMORABLE GAMES

Luton Town, 24 December 1955, White Hart Lane.

My Tottenham debut came in a fixture, which would today seem rather unglamorous, against Luton Town. Back in the mid-fifties, however, the Hatters were an established First Division side. But to be honest, the opposition mattered little, as making my initial appearance for Tottenham was the main thing. An ideal Christmas present.

The White Hart Lane pitch, if I remember rightly, was rather muddy to say the least and playing conditions were always going to be difficult.

The conditions certainly hampered both teams and along with playing with new team mates, I struggled a little bit and did not have the best of afternoon's. I think I troubled the photographers behind the goals more then I troubled the Luton goalkeeper.

Goals from Brooks and Duquemin gave Tottenham a two goal lead, which was reduced by one, when some bad marking allowed Luton to pull one back ten minutes from the end.

My Tottenham career had begun.

West Bromwich Albion, 18 April 1959, White Hart Lane.

Most people associate my time at White Hart Lane with the 'glory glory' days of the early sixties, but it wasn't always like that. Indeed, immediately prior to those memorable seasons, the threat of relegation was very real.

On the final day of season 1958-59 we faced West Bromwich Albion at White Hart Lane and the 5-0 victory made certain that we retained our place in the top flight for at least another twelve months.

We got off to a great start, with a Johnny Brooks goal after seven minutes and from then on, we were never in any danger of losing.

As the record books show, I scored our other four goals in a memorable win. Of the four, the first was the best, with an overhead kick. The others have disappeared from the memory through the years, but they contributed to our remaining in the First Division and I suppose in a way were somewhat instrumental in setting us off on our trail for glory. Had we been relegated, who knows what would have happened?

Arsenal, 16 January 1961, White Hart Lane

Our north London "derbies" were always intense affairs, as they still are today and if I had to pick out one of those games, I would probably go for our 3-0 victory in January 1961.

On an icy pitch, we turned on a superb exhibition of football that had the men of the press scribbling down every adjective that they knew in order to describe our performance.

Little Tommy Harmer you would have thought was on ice skates, the way he tormented the Gunners defence. He set up our first goal about ten minutes after half time, gliding past four players before crossing perfectly for me to slot home.

Tommy had combined with John White early in the game to set up Les Allen for our first and it was the same player who scored our third, after I thought I had scored with a shot on the turn. Much to my disappointment, it rattled off the cross bar.

Such was our performance that afternoon, that many pundits were tipping us strongly to win the Championship, even although it was still only January.

Manchester United, 30 November 1957.

When I joined Tottenham in 1955, Manchester United were, like today, the team that everyone wanted to beat. Fixtures against them required little in the way of motivation.

One particular fixture at Old Trafford, on November 30th 1957, still stands out in my memory. Not just because we beat them 4-3, but because I managed to score a first half hat trick against the best side in the country.

Ok, United were slightly under strength, with no Tommy Taylor or Johnny Berry and young David Gaskell was making his League debut. But after going a goal behind to a David Pegg effort, we took command of the game and stormed into a 4-1 lead at the interval.

Up against Danny Blanchflower's young brother Jackie, I challenged him for a high ball, got a lucky break and ran through to beat Gaskell for the equaliser. That was in the 20th minute and seven minutes later, collecting a pass from Danny Blanchflower out on the left, I chested the ball down before flicking it over the head of Roger Byrne before firing once again past Gaskell for our second.

Our third that afternoon was an own goal by Jackie Blanchflower, who misplaced his back pass to his goalkeeper, as I put him under a little bit of pressure.

MEMORABLE GAMES

Just before the interval, I claimed my hat trick. A Robb centre, if I remember correctly, was misjudged by two United defenders, leaving me with a relatively easy header to score.

After the interval, it was nearly all United, but we managed to keep Duncan Edwards, their main threat, under relatively close control.

David Pegg scored his second to make it 4-2 and with quite a while still to play Liam Whelan made it 4-3. Thankfully, we managed to hold on to our lead as United pressed for the equaliser.

One other thing I remember, was something that we commented on prior to the match, was the fact that the United team that afternoon did not cost a penny to assemble.

Burnley, F. A. Cup Semi-Final, 18 March 1961.

Burnley were certainly not going to provide Tottenham with an easy ninety-minutes in the F. A. Cup semi-final tie at Villa Park. Having lost 4-1 to Hamburg in the European Cup three days previously, it was difficult for us to know what sort of effect the defeat was going to have on them. We also had to remember that they had fought back from being 4-0 down to earn a point at White Hart Lane, earlier in the season.

It took Tottenham half an hour to break the Burnley rearguard down, when I latched onto a defensive error.

The usually competent Jimmy Adamson, somehow missed a through ball by Les Allen and as the ball bounced under his foot, I managed to react quickly enough, racing through to score.

Up until that point, Burnley had looked the better side, but after that goal, we began to take control.

Within a minute of the second half beginning, it looked as if Burnley had drawn level, when Robson headed past Bill Brown, but to our great relief, however, the referee gave us a free kick for pushing by the Burnley forward.

Two minutes later, I scored our second, when I volleyed home from the edge of the penalty area, following an attempted Burnley clearance.

The referee ignored appeals for penalties at either end as we slowly began to wear our opponents down. To their credit though, they kept pressing, but it began to look as though their mid-week defeat had taken quite a bit out of them.

SPURS in ACTION

A pictorial survey of

SEASON
1962 63

A 'WEEKLY HERALD' PUBLICATION

TWO SHILLINGS

MEMORABLE GAMES

With only a minute or so to go, Cliff Jones scored our third and it was a case of 'Wembley here we come'.

Upon the referee's whistle for full time, I was too slow in heading towards the tunnel and was suddenly caught by pitch invading supporters. Hoisting me onto their shoulders, no mean feat in itself, they carried me off the pitch.
So much for the criticism that I had to endure a few weeks previously.

Sheffield Wednesday, White Hart Lane, 17 April 1961

This was not so much of a game to remember, but an occasion to remember, as it saw Tottenham lift the Football League Championship for only the second time.

Sheffield Wednesday were a major obstacle in our Championship path prior to the events of that evening in North London, as a victory would keep their own title hopes alive. A draw, however, was all we required to claim the crown.

Three minutes prior to the interval, it was Wednesday who took the lead. Don Megson, one of their full backs, hammering home a rebound from a free kick.
Our nerves were showing, as half time approached with Wednesday having also hit the post.

Somewhat against the run of play and with the referee looking at his watch, a long clearance from our defence, Peter Baker I think it was, was headed on by Terry Dyson towards me. With two touches, I had the ball in the back of the Wednesday net. My first touch lifted it over the head of Peter Swan, while my second saw the ball fly past Ron Springett into the net.

The cheers from our supporters were still echoing down Tottenham Road, when we scored again. Les Allen hitting a Maurice Norman header home.

The second half failed to live up to that frantic four minutes before the interval, but it was going to take two goals from Wednesday to deprive us of that title. Two goals which were never likely to materialise against the Champions.

The match did have something of a sour note to it, as I was involved in an unintentional collision with Wednesday goalkeeper Ron Springett. Some felt that I was a little robust, but Ron treated it as an accident and part and parcel of the game and we left the pitch arm in arm.

MEMORABLE GAMES

Leicester, F. A. Cup Final, 6 May 1961.

Already League Champions, we were ninety minutes away from history.

I have already detailed my Cup Final dilemma elsewhere, but my pre-match escapade was well worth it in the end, as I scored one of our goals and helped create history.

Eight minutes was all the time it took for us to win that Final and re-write the history books, with two goals scored between the sixty-ninth and seventy-seventh minutes.

Les Allen and John White missed easy opportunities early in the game, while Cliff Jones thought he had given us the lead in the thirty-eight minute, but a linesman's flag cancelled it out. There was nothing, however, to deprive me of my sixty-ninth minute strike.

With only a limited space, I managed to turn quickly before shooting past Banks for our opener.

I also had a hand in our second, taking the ball to the touchline before centring to Terry Dyson to head home.

Leicester's opportunities were restricted due to an injury to Len Chalmers, but I do not think that even with eleven fit men they would have prevented us from lifting the Cup.

Switzerland away 1957.

My last memorable match is included, not because it won us a trophy – it didn't. Or because I scored four goals – I did. The reason that I place it alongside the others, is because it was a game that saw Tottenham beat the full Swiss international side. Our 5-4 victory even overshadowed Scotland's narrow 2-1 victory some weeks previously.

It was, as the score suggests, a closely fought encounter.

I put Tottenham two in front in the 26th and 34th minute, but our hosts, however, fought back after their initial surprise in going behind, scoring thrice in the last ten minutes of the first half.

As the second half got underway, Switzerland kept the pressure on, hitting the bar before increasing their lead to 4-2.

Just on the hour I nabbed my hat trick, which put us back in the game, while ten minutes or so later, Dave Dunmore netted a fourth, making it all square.

It began to look as though the game was going to remain all-square, but with something like five minutes to go, a fine passing movement saw me claim my fourth, Tottenham's fifth and bring an end to a nine goal thriller.

Spurs, League Champions 1961

Ewood Park, Smith, held by Leyland of Blackburn Rovers, Febuary 1960

Chapter 4

THE DOUBLE AND BEYOND

When we kicked off season 1960-61 against Everton at White Hart Lane, neither I or any of my team mates had any idea as to what lay ahead over the next nine months.

I scored our second in a 2-0 win over the 'Toffee's', in that opening fixture, adding a further seven in the next four games, which included a hat trick against Blackpool. This took my total to one hundred and forty one in five years, breaking George Hunt's record of one hundred and thirty eight, set in the pre-wars years. Obviously this gave me a lot of pleasure, as I had already equalled Ted Harpers scoring record of thirty-six League goals for a season during 1957-58.

Not only had I got off to an excellent start in the League, but so had the team as a whole, winning eleven consecutive games. Manchester City ending our run with a 1-1 draw at White Hart Lane in mid-October, when I scored my fourteenth goal of the campaign.

Our first defeat, and one of only seven throughout the season didn't come until November 12th, when Sheffield Wednesday beat us 2-1 at Hillsborough.

We immediately got back to our winning ways, thrashing Birmingham City 6-0 at White Hart Lane. My contribution being a simple penalty. A further run of seven unbeaten games kept us in top position with a reasonable lead.

During February and March, which also saw us heavily involved in the F. A. Cup, we stuttered along, with our eight point lead being whittled down to three, following three defeats, two draws and two wins during that time. Twelve goals in three games, against Chelsea, 4-2 and 3-2, and Preston, 5-0, got us back on track though.

A 3-2 win at Birmingham saw the title move within touching distance and if we could beat Sheffield Wednesday at home, on April 17th, the Championship would be ours.

Played under the White Hart Lane floodlights, we needed all our skills and determination against a strong Sheffield Wednesday side, who were not an easy side to get the better off in those days. Peter Swan, their centre half always giving me a good game.
I remember that the atmosphere was intense, with things heating up further when Wednesday took the lead following a rather controversial free kick. Not long afterwards, they even hit the post.

That seemed to give us a jolt and just before the interval, I grabbed the equaliser.

A long clearance out of defence was surprisingly won in the air by Terry Dyson, who was not the tallest of players, with his header coming in my direction. As the aforementioned Peter Swan came towards me, I managed to flick the ball over his head, move round him before hitting the ball into the roof of the net with my left foot. I was then quickly engulfed by team mates and can remember the crowd going wild with excitement.

Before Wednesday could get themselves re-organised, we were in front.
Another ball high into their penalty area was headed on by Maurice Norman for Les Allen to score the goal which was to win us the Championship.

The scoreline remained at 2-1 and the title was ours, with three games left to play. Little did it matter that we actually lost two of those three.

One of the reasons for the two defeats and the most plausible one was that we were involved in the F. A. Cup Final, with none of us wanting to risk injury in unimportant League games, where the outcome mattered little.

Our F. A. Cup campaign had begun in London, where it would finish, with a home tie against Charlton Athletic, a game we won 3-2.

The fourth round brought nightmares in areas of Cheshire, with Crewe coming out of the old velvet bag immediately after us. This time, however, we could only score five in a 5-1 win! I scored our second.

Aston Villa away were our fifth round opponents and we managed a 2-0 victory, which took us into the quarter finals and three steps from Wembley.

A trip home to the north-east to face Sunderland proved to be our toughest match of the cup campaign and we did well to get a 1-1 draw. The replay, however, was an entirely different story, as we won comfortably 5-0. Once again, I scored our second.

Villa Park was our semi-final venue, with our fellow Championship challengers of the previous season, Burnley, providing the opposition.

Confidence was still high despite a 3-2 defeat in the League against Cardiff City seven days earlier, which was only our fourth of the season, but it was still a fixture that we should have won.

Anyway, against Burnley, play swung from end to end, but around the half-hour mark, I latched on to a bouncing ball just as Jimmy Adamson attempted to clear and drove the ball, right footed, past their goalkeeper.

It was certainly a crucial goal for Tottenham, but it was also one that gave me a lot of pleasure and helped my confidence, as I had been going through something of a lean spell, with a lot of finger pointing going on in my direction. It gave me a lift just at the right time.

Burnley thought that they had levelled through Robson early in the second half, but the goal was disallowed and from then on the game was ours.

THE DOUBLE AND BEYOND

Danny Blanchflower swung a free kick into the Burnley box soon afterwards, that was weakly cleared by one of their defenders. Once again though, I was in the right place at the right time, with the ball landing nicely for me to volley home with my trusty right foot from just inside the penalty box.

Cliff Jones scored our third. We were going to Wembley.

Playing at Wembley in an F. A. Cup Final is every footballers ambition, or should I say was, before the whole thing became too commercialised and the grand old stadium became a thing of the past.

My Cup Final dreams, however, almost became a nightmare, with the chances of me missing out on what was the biggest match in my career to date being quite a distinct possibility.

In our final League match of the season, against West Bromwich Albion at home, a game which saw me score my twenty-eighth goal of the season from thirty-six outings, I twisted my knee. It was obviously painful, but it did not cause me any undue worry. That was, until a light training session a couple of days prior to the Final, when I kicked a ball and at once felt a terrible pain in that same knee.

Thankfully, I managed to complete the session without any further problems and without anyone discovering my 'secret'.

We had another training session pencilled in for Friday, the day before the Final, when the manager would assess any knocks and bruises. So, I had a couple of days to make a miraculous recovery.
Before this session, I went to see my own doctor in Palmers Green, explaining the situation. Reluctantly, he gave me a pain killing injection, which he assured me would see me through any light training. Thankfully, everything went without any hitches and I gave Bill Nicholson no cause for concern.

My doctor had told me to visit him again on the Friday night and much to my horror asked me to return on the morning of the Final and then again around lunch time. This caused me more concern than the actual match itself, as the entire squad were booked into Hendon Hall hotel from the Friday. How the hell was I going to sneak away and get back into London, especially on the Saturday morning?

My room mate at Hendon Hall was Maurice Norman and when he awoke on the Saturday morning to find my bed empty, he had no idea where I was or if I had even slept in it.

I had in fact got up at seven o'clock, climbed out of the window, (thankfully we were on the ground floor) and drove into London for my first injection.

FINAL TIE
LEICESTER CITY
v
TOTTENHAM HOTSPUR

SATURDAY, MAY 6th, 1961   KICK-OFF 3 p.m.

EMPIRE STADIUM
WEMBLEY

OFFICIAL PROGRAMME · ONE SHILLING

Obviously I had to return to the hotel, if only to show my face and when I did so, was immediately cornered by Maurice, wondering where on earth I had been. Pulling him to one side I quickly made him aware of the situation, begging him not to say a word to anyone.

We passed the time reading the various morning newspapers and watching television, but just before our scheduled lunch, I told our trainer, Cecil Poynton, that I was going for a walk to calm the old nerves.

Jumping unseen into my car, I quickly drove as fast as I could back to Palmers Green for my second injection, returning to the hotel minutes after everyone else had sat down to eat. No one suspected anything untoward. I was now ready for Wembley.

Our opponents in the Cup Final and standing between us and a place in the history books, were Leicester City. We had beaten them 2-0 at Filbert Street, when I scored both, but they had gained revenge at the beginning of February by beating us 3-2 at White Hart Lane.

Having won the League, we were obviously favourites, but in a one off match, especially a Cup Final, anything could happen.

In the opening stages of the Wembley show piece, Leicester were clearly the better team and perhaps if they had not suffered an injury to Len Chalmers, one of their full backs, in the nineteenth minute then they might have caused us a few problems. As it was, Chalmers spent the majority of the afternoon limping ineffectively on the wing.

The game plodded on and it was not until the sixty-ninth minute that we finally got the better of Leicester, when a fine passing movement from defence to attack ended with me hitting the ball on the turn past Gordon Banks to give Tottenham the lead.

From then on, there was only one winner and we began to play more confidently, scoring a second with around thirteen minutes still to play.

Les Allen, who I think it was passed to me. I in turn played a one-two with John White, before crossing to where Terry Dyson was waiting to head home.

The double was ours. We had re-written the record books and my clandestine visits to my doctor had thankfully paid off.

(R-L) Tottenham Hotspur manager Bill Nicholson talks to his players: Bobby Smith, Danny Blanchflower, Jimmy Greaves, John White, Peter Baker, Terry Medwin and Cliff Jones

EUROPEAN CUP

Semi-Final, Second Leg

TOTTENHAM HOTSPUR

VERSUS

BENFICA

(PORTUGAL)

**OFFICIAL
PROGRAMME
6d.**

Thursday, 5th April, 1962
Kick-off 7.45 p.m.

Chapter 5

INTO EUROPE AND WEMBLEY AGAIN

As Champions, entry into the European Cup gave us new horizons to pursue and discover and new challenges to meet. We were confident of doing well, while at the same time defending our domestic League and Cup trophies.

Our foreign adventures had to begin in the preliminary round, being newcomers onto the European scene and were drawn against Gornik Zabrze, with the first leg away.

Looking back, perhaps we were a little naive, as in front of 70,000 in Poland, we found ourselves 4-0 down early in the second half. Fortunately, we managed to pull back a couple of goals back before the end, but we had learned our lesson.

With nothing to lose in the return leg the following week, we were prepared to gamble everything on attack, as hitting the post after only thirty seconds clearly emphasised.

By the twentieth minute, we had drawn level on aggregate and eventually won 8-1 on the night.

Feyenoord were our opponents in the first round and we dealt quite confidently with the Dutch side, winning 4-2 on aggregate. I missed the first leg through injury and with no real urgency, or need to play in the game, I didn't bother about visiting my doctor.

The second round took us back to Eastern Europe, to face Dukla Prague. Losing the first leg in Czechoslovakia 1-0, despite now having in the side a player, who was to become a big friend, Jimmy Greaves. We managed to turn the tie around on a snow covered White Hart Lane, winning 4-1. I scored twice.

The atmosphere on those European nights was electric, with the crowd really getting behind us. You couldn't fail to perform with that kind of backing.

We were now in the semi-finals, with Benfica, the current European Cup holders, between us and a place in another Final.

The Portuguese side scored in the opening minutes of the first leg tie in Lisbon, adding a second before the interval, while we struggled a little after having a goal disallowed only one minute after they took the lead.

INTO EUROPE AND WEMBLEY AGAIN

As the second half got underway, I managed to pull a goal back and we began to look capable of taking something from the game. A third Benfica goal soon dashed such thoughts.
I thought that I had once again pulled a goal back, only to have the referee disallow it for offside, even although to this day, I can see the two defenders standing on the goal line.

Although 3-1 down, it was widely thought that we still had a chance of winning the tie. An early Benfica goal, however, presented us with a real up hill task. Once again, I produced the goods, pulling a goal back, but we still required another two to earn a replay.

We had a goal once again disallowed for offside, before Danny Blanchflower scored with a penalty almost immediately after half time. We then threw everything at them, but to Benfica's credit, they managed to hold out.

Despite our efforts in Europe, we did our best to retain the League Championship but at the end of the season we had to be content with third place, one point behind Burnley and four behind Champions Ipswich Town.

Retention of the F. A. Cup was obviously almost as big a priority as the Championship.

Fortunately, this went more according to plan.

The third round draw took us north to Birmingham, where two Jimmy Greaves goals and another from Cliff Jones gave us what we thought was enough to win the game. Goals on either side of half time brought Birmingham back into it and they scrambled an equaliser late into the game.

Birmingham took the lead in the replay, but goals from Terry Medwin, with a double, Jimmy Greaves and Les Allen sealed the tie for us despite Birmingham scoring again.

Plymouth in round four caused us no problems and we ran out 5-1 winners.

It was back to the Midlands for round five and a visit to West Bromwich Albion, where I managed at last to open my Cup scoring account. Better late than never I suppose.

My early goal settled us down and I scored a second before the interval. They managed to pull one back, but my old mate Greavsie scored twice, with Albion managing one in between, to give us a 4-2 win.

INTO EUROPE AND WEMBLEY AGAIN

A 2-0 win over Aston Villa made it a trio of Midlands scalps and we were in the semi-finals.

Our opponents, Manchester United, were still in something of a transitional period following the Munich Air Disaster and never really caused us any problems at Hillsborough. We won 3-1 and I made the first for Jimmy Greaves. Cliff Jones and Terry Medwin, scoring the others.

In the Final, we faced Burnley, our league rivals from over the past few seasons.

Three minutes into the game I got my head to the ball and nodded it down to Jimmy Greaves to engineer our first.

Rather surprisingly, the score line remained the same until five minutes after the interval and it was Burnley who claimed the next goal.

Shaken by this setback, we upped the pace and almost immediately retained the advantage.

Danny Blanchflower passed to John White, who played a one-two with Cliff Jones before crossing the ball into the Burnley penalty area.

Although not the lightest person on my feet, nor noted for my ball control, the Wembley surface was a delight to play on, bringing out the best in you.

Collecting 'the Ghosts' cross, I swivelled before hitting a peach of a shot past Adam Blacklaw in the Burnley goal.

Ten minutes or so from the end, Danny Blanchflower scored from the spot to give me my second F. A. Cup winners medal.

Danny Blanchflower (left) & Bobby Smith - Tottenham Hotspur, hold the cup
as Terry Dyson nips underneath with Bill Brown (goalkeeper far left),
Tottenham Hotspur v Burnley, FA Cup Final 1962.

Tottenham Hotspur with the European Cup Winners' Cup 1963
(back row, l-r) Cliff Jones, Ron Henry, Mel Hopkins, Maurice Norman, John Hollowbread,
Bill Brown, Bobby Smith, John White, Jimmy Greaves, John Smith.
(front row, l-r) Frank Saul, Peter Baker, Dave Mackay, Danny Blanchflower, Tony Marchi, Les Allen, Terry Dyson, Eddie Clayton

Bobby (back row, second from left) at an Eighties reunion with his old team mates

Chapter 6

TRIUMPH IN EUROPE
A Result in Rotterdam

Our European activities for season 1962-63 were scheduled for the European Cup Winners Cup, with the experiences of the previous season proving extremely valuable.

Granted a bye in the first round, the second round draw didn't have much of a European feel about it, but it certainly had plenty of spice, as we were paired with Glasgow Rangers. Drawn at home in the first leg, we gained the advantage in the 'Battle of Britain' with a 5-2 win.

John White opened the scoring in the fourth minute, while Rangers drew level through Henderson.

Towards the end of the first half, Les Allen increased our advantage, before Bobby Shearer deflected the ball into his own net. Rangers, however, pulled one back before the interval. A Maurice Norman goal early in the second half gave us a 5-2 lead to take to Glasgow.

In front of a hugely partisan 80,000 crowd, Greavsie increased our aggregate lead after eight minutes and it wasn't until the second half that Rangers managed to pull one back. The tie was concluded when I scored twice, although the Scottish Cup winners scored another in between.

Slovan Bratislava brought a two goal advantage to London following the first leg of the quarter final and in all honesty, it could have been more.

The return leg at White Hart Lane was, however, a completely different story.
In the opening minutes, I challenged their 'keeper, as I was apt to do in those days and from then on he was a nervous wreck. Strangely, a similar ploy in the first leg had failed to work.

We bombarded the Bratislava goal and by the end of the night had scored six without reply. I only managed one, while Jimmy Greaves grabbed a couple, with Mackay, White and Jones the others.

Our opponents in the semi final were OFK Belgrade, who had taken three games to dispose of Naples in the previous round, but were going to find us a completely different type of team.

I remember that they were a rather physical side, or at least adopted that style in an attempt to put us off our game. There was no way that it would work, as the likes of Dave Mackay and myself enjoyed the odd physical encounter from time to time.

In Yugoslavia, some of their tackles were a bit naughty and it was one rather crude challenge on yours truly, which lead to our first goal.

I was upended on the edge of their penalty area by their centre half and let's just say I didn't take too kindly to it. Once order was restored, I laid the free kick off to John White for our first goal.

Belgrade continued to try and unsettle us and within ten minutes of the second half getting underway, Jimmy Greaves was sent off for a bit of retaliation. This earned him the honour of becoming the first Tottenham player to be sent off in thirty-five years. Despite the ten men, Terry Dyson scored a second with twenty minutes still to play, to give us a 2-0 lead.

The return leg passed peacefully, with goals from Dave Mackay and Cliff Jones finishing off the game as a competitive fixture, before I added a third with a diving header, minutes after half time. Belgrade managed to grab a consolation, but we were in the Final, where our opponents were the holders, Atletico Madrid.

Our plans took a knock prior to the game, with Dave Mackay failing a fitness test, but any worries were soon cast aside.

Jimmy Greaves hit the post early on, which helped our confidence, while half an hour later we were 2-0 in front. A four man move between Blanchflower, White, myself and Jones ended with that man Greaves scoring the first. John White added the second.

Madrid clawed themselves back into the game with a penalty and threatened for a while, before Terry Dyson restored our two goal advantage.

Jimmy Greaves scored his second and our fourth, as we strolled towards the final whistle and Britain's first European triumph. Terry Dyson scored again to make it 5-1 with the best goal of the night, a twenty-five yard drive, three minutes from the end.

I recall telling him at full time that he should retire, as he would never play a better game.

Bill Nicholson

Chapter 7
MANAGEMENT STYLES

Bill Nicholson

Although things ended on a bit of a sour note, I had great admiration for the man who had the belief in me when he signed me from Chelsea. Although at the time Bill was assistant manager.

One thing that I particularly liked about him was the fact that he trusted the players and treated us like mature adults. He also taught us respect and his organisational skills were second to none.

Tottenham Hotspur owe him so much, as do the players of the double era, as without the guidance of Bill Nicholson, the club's honours board would have a few blank spaces and the players of that time would not be remembered fondly by the supporters of today.

Walter Winterbottom

My England manager on the other hand was very different to Bill. He was more into the coaching side of things, with the actual team selection initially down to the selectors.

Perhaps having only been a bit player at Manchester United prior to World War Two, stepping into the Director of Coaching role with the F.A. and then the England set up saw him miss out on quite a bit of experience.

Perhaps if I had more involvement with him, instead of just odd days, then I would have been able to get to know him a bit more.

Of the other managers, Matt Busby made a big impression, as he did with everyone, creating that amazing team that perished at Munich and then rebuilding the side into the memorable side of the Sixties with Best, Law and Charlton.

Finney farewell. Tom Finney in his last game v Luton. 30 April 1960

Chapter 7
MY TALENTED CONTEMPORARIES

John Charles

What a player. Whether playing centre half or centre forward, Big John was an outstanding individual, revered both in Britain with Leeds United and Wales and in Italy with Juventus.

He was awesome in the air, with no-one getting the better of him throughout the course of the game.

Players such as John Charles come along only once in a blue moon and they are a joy to watch and hell to play against.

John was not just a great player and a difficult opponent, he was also a gentleman and a pleasure to know.

Tom Finney

Incomparable. For me the most gifted English forward of all time and a better all round player than Matthews. A definite match winner was the 'Preston Plumber'.

Not only was Tom a goal maker, plying regularly on the wing, he was also a goal taker, often employing a deep lying centre forward role.

His consistency earned him the Footballer of the Year award twice in three years, in 1954 and 1957. Another footballing gentleman, still held in awe today.

Stanley Matthews

Stan was the other half of the great footballing debate of "Who is or was the best, Matthews or Finney". A debate which still simmers away today. I have already cast my vote.

Stan, like Tom Finney, lovely man to know who enjoyed a career that seemed to stretch for a lot more than thirty- three years.

Thankfully, I did not play full back, as I would never have relished a confrontation with Stan, or with Tom for that matter, as he mesmerised more full backs than I seemed to score goals.

Like his arch rival, Stan was also voted Footballer of the Year twice, although his awards were not so close together - 1948 and 1963, while his fame and ability also stretched to the continent, winning the European Footballer of the Year award in 1956.

MY TALENTED CONTEMPORARIES

Bobby Charlton

Another player whom I admired was Bobby Charlton, whose performances in the white of England are perhaps just as memorable as those with United. He actually scored one of our goals on my England debut, against Northern Ireland on October 8th 1960 and seven days later scored a hat trick, as did my old Tottenham mate Jimmy Greaves, in my second game against Luxembourg.

Both players confining my own double strike to a mere mention in the following days match reports.

An inspiration on and off the park for United, Bobby did not command the same attention as say Best and Law in the Sixties and Viollet before them, but if you ever gave him a sniff of the goal, then you could expect to be punished.

A huge influence to United following the Munich Air disaster, something that he took some time to recover from.

He wasn't a great scorer of goals, but a scorer of great goals.

Duncan Edwards

Professional footballers, like supporters, have players whom they admire. Talented individuals whom they hope do not have an inspired ninety minutes against their own particular team.

When coming face to face with such a player, the inspiration to do well is perhaps greater, in the hope that your game can rise to the same level as theirs and success, if only for one afternoon can be achieved.

Over the course of my career I came into opposition with many footballers from a period when there were possibly more players of note than there are today. However, if I had to chose the one who gained my admiration more than any other, there would be little deliberation, that player would be Duncan Edwards of Manchester United.

There is little that I can say about Duncan that has not been said before, but for me he was the complete footballer. There was nothing that he couldn't do, and do well. Everything seemed to come naturally to him.

I was privileged to play against him on a few occasions, enjoying the competitiveness of our confrontations, although I was always thankful that we were never in direct opposition.

MY TALENTED CONTEMPORARIES

There were some players against whom you could perhaps gain some advantage by being slightly more forceful in your play, but against Duncan, such a ploy would have been wasted. His physical strength was incomparable and any such tactics would have given him even more determination to come out on top.

One minute he could take the ball from you in a hard but always fair challenge. The next, he would be in your penalty area at the opposite end of the ground looking for a goal.

For me, Duncan Edwards was faultless, with his death dealing a huge blow to both Manchester United and England. If it hadn't been for the Munich Air disaster, I could have possibly enjoyed the privilege of playing with him in the white of England.

Two days after the crash I stood, along with the players of Manchester City, observing a minutes silence and the hat trick I scored that afternoon did little to ease the memories of those United lads who had died. My thoughts during that pre match tribute also drifted to Germany, where Duncan lay badly injured in hospital.

Sadly, I was never to enjoy playing against my favourite player again.

Alfredo Di Stefano

An Argentine, who also played for Spain, Di Stefano ranks high in many players from my era's selection of top favourite individuals.

He was a part of the Real Madrid 'super team' of the late nineteen fifties, early nineteen sixties, winning five European Cup medals and forming an exciting partnership with the likes of Puskas and Gento, thrilling countless supporters across the world.

I remember watching that memorable European Cup Final at Hampden Park Glasgow, in 1960, when Real simply overwhelmed Eintracht Frankfurt 7-3. A match still considered on of the best ever played in Britain. You couldn't fail to be inspired by Di Stefano's brilliance.

The masterly ball player was a stocky built individual, but carried a wealth of talent, making him one of the world's all time greats, emphasised by his European Cup scoring record of forty-nine goals in fifty-eight games.

Johnny Haynes

The man who opened the way for bigger pay packets for footballers, when he became the first one hundred pound per week player.

An excellent inside forward, whose range of passing skills were second to none and a player whom I had the pleasure of playing alongside for England.

Perhaps he didn't get on the score sheet too often when we played together for our country, but he certainly made telling contributions to the goals that I managed to score.

A dedicated one club man and an inspiration to any young player back in the Fifties and Sixties.

Tommy Taylor

A first class striker and a player who would have been England's no.9 for a long time, had it not been for the Munich Air Disaster. My own chances would probably have been limited in the England set up if Tommy's career had not come to an untimely and unfortunate end.

A powerfully built front man, not too unlike myself, who was equally capable of scoring with his head as he was with his feet and it was no surprise that Matt Busby felt strongly enough to pay almost £30,000 to Barnsley for him.

Tommy was a real handful for any centre half and was not frightened to go in where it hurt in an attempt to get on the scoresheet.

Frank McLintock

Despite the man being a 'Gunner', I had great admiration for the Scottish internationalist centre half. A man who led Arsenal to much success in the nineteen seventies.

Frank was not big in build but he made up for it in leadership and stamina and was also a good reader of the game.

He was a different type of captain to Danny Blanchflower, but like my old Tottenham team mate, he could get the best out of his players as they jointly fought for success.

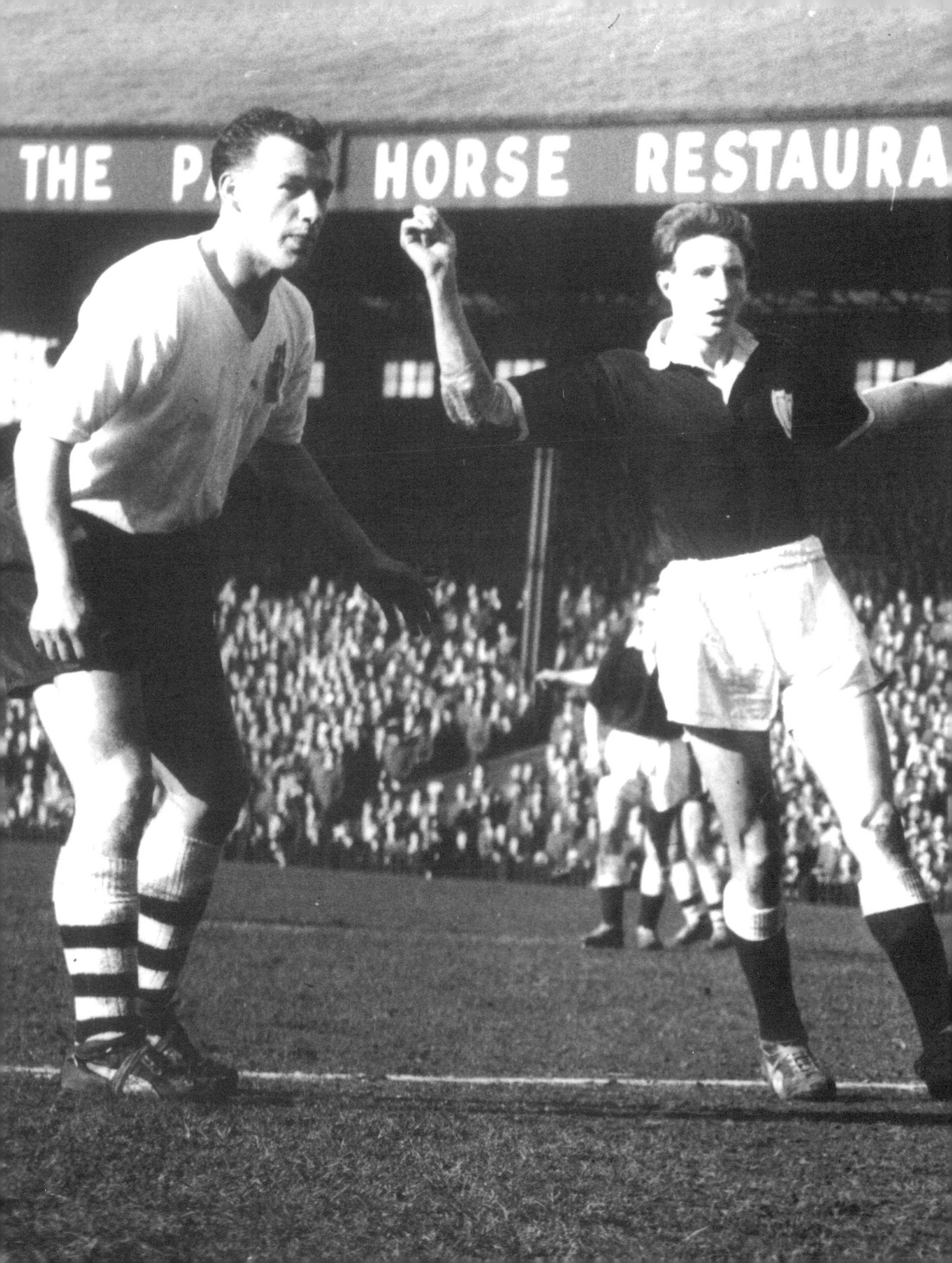
THE PA HORSE RESTAURA

Jimmy McIlroy

One of the best creative inside forwards in the business. He was one of the main reasons behind Burnley's successful period in the early Sixties, combining with Jimmy Adamson in the Turf Moor club's engine room.

Like many inside forwards over the years, there was not much physically to him, but there was always danger when he was around, with his skill not only beneficial to the likes of Burnley and later Stoke City, but also to Northern Ireland.

Nat Lofthouse

Like Tommy Taylor, a real powerhouse of a centre forward who found the back of the net regularly for both Bolton Wanderers and England.

Jackie Milburn

A member of that famous footballing family, which also produced Bobby and Jack Charlton and a man whose name is still a legend on Tyneside.

If I thought that my two F. A. Cup winners medals were a big achievement, then I was clearly outclassed by 'Wor Jackie' who won three, scoring in two of those Finals.

A one club man, playing all his football for Newcastle United, where he played over three hundred and fifty games, scoring one short of one hundred and eighty goals.

Another player who would fit in to the category of a footballing gentleman.

England's Bobby Smith warming up at the Bank of England training ground in Roehampton

Chapter 9

A NEW WHITE SHIRT

I was on the golf course at Crews Hill near Enfield when I received the news of my initial England call up, to face Northern Ireland in Belfast in October 1960. Tottenham manager, Bill Nicholson, knowing where I was, phoning the clubhouse to pass on the news.

My goals for Tottenham had catapulted me towards the fringe of the England side and I suppose the selectors thought it was worth giving me a run out to see what I could do.

I was certainly in the best form of my career, having began pre season training three weeks early and also lost a bit of weight.

So, my international career began in Northern Ireland, replacing Brian Clough in the number nine shirt and I could not have dreamt of a better start, scoring once in our 5-2 win.

Obviously, it was now difficult for the selectors to leave me out of the next match, having performed reasonably well and I did indeed keep my place, playing against Luxembourg eleven days later.

Once again I did my international ambitions a lot of good, this time scoring twice, as we overwhelmed our lesser opponents 9-0.

The following week came my big test, Spain at Wembley. Perhaps it was the rain soaked pitch that affected the Spaniards, but we completely outplayed them to win 4-2. Once again, I scored twice.

My second was an exquisite chip from fully twenty-five yards out and the following day I seemed to have captured most of the newspaper headlines.

"Smith Forges A Brand New England" is one that I recall, while another reporter wrote that I was worth two Di Stefano's that afternoon. This was particularly pleasing, even although it was a bit off the mark as the Real Madrid man was a truly world class individual. However, at the end of the game he did come over and congratulate me on my two goals.

My scoring touch continued, with three goals in my next two games, against Wales and Scotland. The latter was that game that all Scots want to forget, the 9-3 trouncing at Wembley.

Missing the visit of Mexico to Wembley, I returned to face Portugal, but failed to continue my fine scoring run. I then found myself omitted from the side for the next seven games. An appearance in Glasgow against Scotland was followed by another nine games without my name appearing on the team sheet and it then took me four games to claim my next England goal, against Czechoslovakia in Bratislava and a 4-2 win.

I kept my place for the second of what was an end of season three game tour, stepping down for Johnny Byrne in the third.

Against Wales, in Cardiff, the next England international, I scored twice and following an appearance against the Rest of the World, I scored my thirteenth international goal against Northern Ireland.

This, however, was to prove unlucky, as it was my last international appearance as my whole career took a turn for the worse.

Bobby's England badge
from one of his England shirts

Greaves on attack April 1965

Chapter 10

A GENIUS CALLED GREAVSIE

Without reservation Jimmy Greaves was simply the greatest goalscoring machine that I have ever seen.

Jimmy joined Chelsea a couple of years after I had left the club, but the stories of this phenomenal kids scoring attributes at Stamford Bridge were endless. In his first year as a sixteen year old amateur, he amassed over 100 goals in all levels of football in a single season and it was no surprise when Chelsea announced that he was to be released into the hurly-burly traumas of the old First Division.

I was part of the Spurs team that watched in amazement as this spiky haired kid with the baggy shorts make his Chelsea debut at White Hart Lane in August of 1957. He literally ran us ragged and finished a breathtaking inaugural match with a wonderful equaliser. It was the prelude to a brilliant Chelsea career that saw him score an unbelievable 132 goals in a mere 169 appearances for the Blues.

Following his departure from Chelsea. we heard of his unhappy spell in Italian football and of the interest that Spurs had shown in bringing him back to England, but manager Bill Nicholson always kept his negotiations like the proverbial playing cards close to his chest. Even though we had just completed the amazing Double, the news that Jimmy Greaves was to become a Tottenham Hotspur player in November 1961 was simply amazing.

He started with a bang, notching three goals in his Tottenham debut against Blackpool and finished his first season, (which remember only stretched from December to May) with 30 goals in 29 Cup and League appearances.

He was a unique talent, easy to play with and our telepathic understanding created havoc with many First Division and European defences. I remember in the Semi-final and final of the 1962 FA Cup competition laying off two deft passes that left Jimmy with the opportunity to score the goals as only great players like he can.

We played together for a majority of my 15 England games and took that unique goalpoaching understanding on to the international fields. In Season 1960 - 61 we broke all records with the following winning results : Northern Ireland away 5-2, Luxembourg away 9-0, Spain 4-2, Wales 5-1 and Scotland 9-2. We scored an amazing 32 goals in those five matches with Jimmy and myself sharing 17 of them.

They were great times at Tottenham in those Glory, Glory days of the 60's, and playing with Blanchflower, Mackay, Jones and the other members of that Super Spurs side was my highlight of a wonderful career. But striking for goal with a genius like Jimmy Greaves was extra special. Like many other of his team mates, at both club and international level, I always thought that before we played with him he was a lucky player, that somehow the deflected shot or pass was fortunate enough to find its way through to him.

A GENIUS CALLED GREAVSIE

How wrong you can be. He had a natural goal poachers instinct for being in the right place at the right time. And never let it be said that he wasn't brave. To score 411 goals, and all in the rigours of the old first division where brutish defenders where licensed to kick , believe me you had to have bravery in the Victoria Cross class.

That says it all about a genius called Jimmy Greaves.

Bobby in 1958

Chapter 11

THE WORLD CUP
Teddy and Me

I felt a common bond with current Tottenham favourite Teddy Sheringham, as he left with the England World Cup party for Japan and Korea, as it took me back to Sweden in 1958.

Then, like Teddy, I was a star at White Hart Lane, but found myself going off to the World Cup as very much a back-up man. In my case, it was even more so than in Teddy's.

My call up into the England squad for the Finals, in Sweden, was in reality just to make up the numbers. To be completely honest, if it had not been for the Munich Air Disaster, I would never have been selected at all.

Tommy Taylor was England's number one choice centre forward and had been, for a couple of years. Regularly finding the back of the net, scoring sixteen goals in nineteen games.

His sad and untimely death, along with that of Roger Byrne and Duncan Edwards was a major factor in England's poor performances upon the world stage in Sweden.

As it was, West Bromwich Albion's Derek Kevan stepped into the vacant number nine shirt, playing in the four games prior to the tournament, scoring thrice. I was more than grateful just to be called into the squad as a back up player.

Although it was nice to be involved, it was disappointing that England failed to win any of their three games, losing one and drawing three. Perhaps if the USSR, in the group play off had not beaten us, I might have got my chance if we had gone through. As it was, we were knocked out, without me having kicked a ball.

Derek Kevan scored in two of those games, but surprisingly, in the first match following the World Cup, the number nine shirt went to Bobby Charlton, with three others players filling that position before I got my chance.

I also suffered disappointment in 1962, when I was left out of the squad that went to Chile, despite playing in two of the qualifying matches against Luxemburg and Portugal. What made matters worse was that I returned to the side following the Finals and continued to score goals.

So, it was an uneasy time for me and that's why I felt some sympathy for Teddy. He went off to Korea and Japan knowing that Owen and Heskey were probably the manager's first choice as the main strikers and that Darius Vassal had scored some important goals in the lead up to the competition.

Teddy, however, did have an advantage over me in that he had played in France '98 and although he didn't score, he did get to play on the ultimate stage during his wonderful career.

Despite my disappointment of forty years earlier, at least I can say that I was there.

Tottenham's Stephen Carr, while playing for the Republic of Ireland, clears under pressure from Portugal's Pedro Bardossa

Tottenham's Robbie Keane (r), while playing for the Republic of Ireland, tries to bend the ball around the Germany defensive wall

Chapter 12
THE YOUNG COCKERELS

Ledley King

I have been very impressed with Ledley in the early days of his Tottenham career.

The big Londoner, very mobile for a player of his build, has erased the memory of Sol Campbell and I can see him being a prominent fixture in the side for many years to come.

Ledley is also a certainty for a regular place in the full England side, having already made his senior debut.

Stephen Carr

Continuing the long running vein of fine full backs at White Hart Lane, Stephen Carr makes up for his lack of height with skill and determination.

I particularly warm to the attacking part of his game and would like to see him score more goals similar to the twenty five yard screamer that he scored against Manchester United in Tottenham's 3-1 win a couple of seasons or so ago.

Alongside Ledley King, they will be key figures in the Tottenham defence for a number of years to come.

Robbie Keane

I was surprised when Leeds allowed Robbie to join Tottenham, as I find him an exciting individual to watch.

Robbie first caught my eye as a Coventry City player whilst watching 'Match of the Day', as his dribbling skills, ball control and goals were a regular feature of the Saturday night programme.

Hopefully, his goals will help bring some success to Tottenham in the near future. He should also reap the rewards from playing alongside Teddy Sheringham.

Gus Poyet

Gus made a big name for himself as a Chelsea player, but also suffered a few injuries that reduced his appearances for the Stamford Bridge side.

However, in many of his appearances, he was the difference between Chelsea and their opponents, scoring goals which I could only dream about.

Tall for a forward, but obviously very good in the air.

Another surprise Tottenham signing, but he added panache and a distinctive flair to a side which for so long was missing someone of his class.

Jamie Redknapp

Another player who has not had the best of luck with injuries, but since joining Tottenham, has returned to something like his best form. Hopefully they can reap the rewards that Liverpool missed out on.

He certainly has the talent to not only re-establish himself at White Hart Lane, but also resurrect his England international career. Perhaps he can do for Tottenham what his manager did for a while a few years ago.

Above: A star studded line up for the
Bill Nicholson Testimonial in 2001.
Bobby is back row, third from right.

Right: Bobby's own Testimonial Dinner
from 1996.

Les Gold
PROMOTIONS

PRESENTS THE

BOBBY SMITH
TESTIMONIAL DINNER

FEATURING
JIMMY GREAVES

PLUS MANY MEMBERS OF THE
SPURS "DOUBLE" WINNING SIDE
TOGETHER WITH OTHER FOOTBALL GREATS

ON THURSDAY 31ST OCTOBER 1996

AT THE STARLIGHT SUITE,
SOUTHBURY ROAD, ENFIELD.

Chapter 13

THE POSTMAN STILL CALLS

It seems that football is now more popular than ever before.

During my playing days, we would frequently perform in front of bigger crowds, sprawled across the vast open terraces, but then, television coverage was practically non-existent compared to the saturated broadcasting of today. In my playing days, the only live match you would find on the box was the F. A. Cup Final.

Radio would give you reasonable coverage, as would the newspapers, but again, the latter was nowhere near the mass coverage of today's tabloids and broadsheets.

In other words, if you wanted to see any football, watch the big name players in action, then you had to go to a game.

The sea of cloth caps alone told you that most of the people there were working men and their sons, letting off steam and escaping from the rigours of their workplace on a Saturday afternoon.

Nowadays, if you go to White Hart Lane, or anywhere else for that matter, you are likely to find yourself sitting next to a doctor or lawyer than a factory worker.

The appeal of the game has spread to everyone in the last ten years or so and it has now become 'trendy' to enjoy football.

Obviously, I feel that football in my day was better. Perhaps we did not have the same level of all round fitness of today's top players, but I often wonder how they would get on with the not so light weight strips and the much heavier boots and ball.

Although it is almost five decades since I began my career with Chelsea, I am always amazed by the amount of mail that I still receive from fans. This has increased enormously over the past few years, with letters now coming in from all over the world, not just North London.

Not surprisingly, most of them are about the 1961 Double winning season, with many coming from people who were not even born at the time.

I am also surprised that it is not just Tottenham Hotspur supporters who remember me with some sort of affection, but also those of Chelsea. I was recently surprised to discover that I was named as one of the Stamford Bridge club's worst ever sales during the nineteen fifties, during a debate on Chelsea TV!

From time to time I manage to meet up with some of my old team mates at dinners or whatever, but it is the supporters who always want to reminisce about the good old 'glory glory' days. Many have amazing memories, recalling incidents, never mind goals.

Many also enjoy collecting memorabilia from days gone by and I am often surprised at some of the items that I am asked to sign.

HALL OF FAME

Bobby Smith

Another personality around whom the team revolves
Was once a yorkshire blacksmith who now hammers in the goals
A powerful centre forward who can score with feet and head
To the toughest of defenders, he's a sight that they all dread
For with his bull like charges as he rushes in to score
No centre half could tame him, it would need a matador
But though he's been capped for england, for his deadly accurate shot
It seems when they need a scapegoat, it's always him they drop
But our bobby has broad shoulders, he still manages to smile
So I acknowledge a great player, bred in the tottenham style

TREVILLION — 63

Chapter 14

BESIDE THE SEASIDE

My days at Tottenham obviously produced the highlights of my career, bringing goals, medals and of course England recognition. But it was also going to bring me disappointment.

The latter came when I realised that manager Bill Nicholson no longer considered me his first choice front man. It wouldn't have been so bad if Tottenham had signed another centre forward, but the manager signed Laurie Brown, a half back from Arsenal to play in my place. A player who had never played up front in the First Division.

I had heard of Brown's signing and thought nothing of it really. But when I was called to the managers office, he told me of his plans.

Not only was my Tottenham career brought to a sudden halt, so was my international one. Ok, I had been out of the Tottenham side with a slight illness, but I was on my way back to full fitness.

Needless to say, I stormed out of the ground after telling Bill Nicholson what I thought.

I eventually left White Hart Lane, signing for Brighton in a £5,000 deal in May 1964 and in my debut for the south coast club attracted their biggest crowd for three seasons. I also marked my debut with two goals.

Although I only played at the Goldstone Ground for one season, my 19 in 31 games helped a bit, as we won the Fourth Division title.

Things began to turn sour when they sacked me for writing a few newspaper articles without permission. Sadly the articles also saw me banned from White Hart Lane due to a few comments I made about the club.

As they say though, time is a great healer and the imposed ban was eventually withdrawn.

My playing career also resumed, as I moved to Southern League Hastings United in October 1965, on a free transfer. I stayed here for around three years, before finishing my career with a brief spell at Banbury United.

Chapter 15
THE GAMES & THE GOALS

Career
- Redcar Boys Club
- Redcar United
- Tudor Rose
- Chelsea groundstaff May, 1949
- Professional May, 1950
- Tottenham Hotspur December, 1955
- Brighton & Hove Albion May, 1964
- Hastings United October, 1965
- Orient trial March, 1967
- Banbury United summer, 1968.

Season	League App	Gls	FA Cup App	Gls	League Cup App	Gls	European App	Gls
1950-51	16	7	5	2				
1951-52	32	11	7	5				
1952-53	7	1						
1953-54	8							
1954-55	4							
1955-56	7	4						
Chelsea	74	23	12	7				
1955-56	21	10	6	3				
1956-57	33	18	3	1				
1957-58	38	36	2	2				
1958-59	36	32	4	3				
1959-60	40	25	4	5				
1960-61	36	28	7	5				
1961-62	26	6	4	3			6	6
1962-63	15	8	1				6	4
1963-64	26	13	1				2	
Tottenham	271	176	32	22			14	10
1964-65	31	19	1		1	1		
1965-66					1	1		
Brighton	31	19	1		1	1		
Total	**376**	**218**	**45**	**29**	**2**	**2**	**14**	**10**

THE GAMES & THE GOALS

Bobby's 208 senior goals for Tottenham were scored against the following clubs:

Club	Goals	Club	Goals
Arsenal	10	Leyton Orient	1
Aston Villa	11	Luton Town	1
Benfica	2	Manchester City	8
Birmingham City	4	Manchester Utd	11
Blackburn Rovers	7	Newcastle Utd	4
Blackpool	12	Newport County	3
Bolton Wand.	11	Nottingham F.	4
Boston United	2	OFK Belgrade	1
Burnley	8	Portsmouth	6
Cardiff City	1	Preston NE	4
Charlton Athletic	1	Rangers	2
Chelsea	10	Sheffield United	5
Crewe Alexandra	5	Sheffield Wed.	4
Doncaster Rovers	1	Slovan Bratislava	1
Dukla Prague	2	Stoke City	1
Everton	11	Sunderland	3
Gornik Zabrze	2	WBA	17
Ipswich Town	1	West Ham Utd	4
Leeds United	6	Wolves	12
Leicester City	9		

Bobby took over as holder of the club record aggregate League goalscorer with the first of his three goals in a 3-1 home win over Blackpool on August 31, 1960. George Hunt had held the record of 124 League goals since March, 1937. Bobby's final tally of 176 League goals remained the club record until Jimmy Greaves overtook him during March, 1968.

Bobby's 36 goal haul in Division One during season 1957-58 equalled the club record set by Ted Harper back in the 1930-31 Second Division campaign. That record stood until Greaves surpassed them both scoring 37 during 1962-63.

GOAL IN A MILLION!

Six-part story of a fantastic moment that had White Hart Lane in a ferment.

The game—Spurs v. Wolves. The scorer—Bobby Smith, of Spurs. The way it happened—

A high ball from the left into Wolves' goalmouth. Up goes Smith. Now—a bicycle kick, speciality of the Continentals.

Over the Spurs' man's shoulder flies the ball as he turns almost a complete somersault.

Bewildered by this quick-fire action, Wolves' 'keeper comes out—too late.

The ball rockets past him into the net as the scorer lands on his back.

What a goal! It was one of four by Smith in a game that finished 5-1 for Spurs.

The scorer in close-up—BOBBY SMITH.

The following eleven hat-trick's, or better, were scored by Bobby during his time with Tottenham. Ten came in First Division matches with the exception being his four goal haul against Crewe in an FA Cup fourth round replay.

28.04.56	v Sheffield United	home	won 3-1	
30.11.57	v Manchester United	away	won 4-3	
08.02.58	v Manchester City	home	won 5-1	
12.03.58	v Bolton Wanderers	home	won 4-1	
29.03.58	v Aston Villa	home	won 6-2	(4)
11.10.58	v Everton	home	won 10-4	(4)
18.04.59	v West Bromwich Albion	home	won 5-0	(4)
10.10.59	v Wolverhampton W.	home	won 5-1	(4)
03.02.60	v Crewe Alexandra	home	won 13-2	(4)
15.04.60	v Chelsea	away	won 3-1	
31.08.60	v Blackpool	home	won 3-1	

International Career

Bobby's international career spanned three years and 43 days, gaining 15 caps and netting 13 goals. He scored in each of his first five internationals and was on the winning side in his first and last five games.

08.10.60 v Northern Ireland at Belfast Won 5-2

Bobby opened the scoring with a powerful shot after 16 minutes in a Home International Championship fixture.

19.10.60 v Luxembourg at Luxembourg Won 9-0

Bobby scored two goals as England comfortably won their opening World Cup qualifying match.

26.10.60 v Spain at Wembley Won 4-2

Bobby Charlton provided the centre for Bobby to steer a 68th minute header goalwards to put England 3-2 ahead. A clever lob twelve minutes later secured his second goal.

23.11.60 v Wales at Wembley Won 5-1

Bobby notched England's third goal towards the end of the first half of this Home International game.

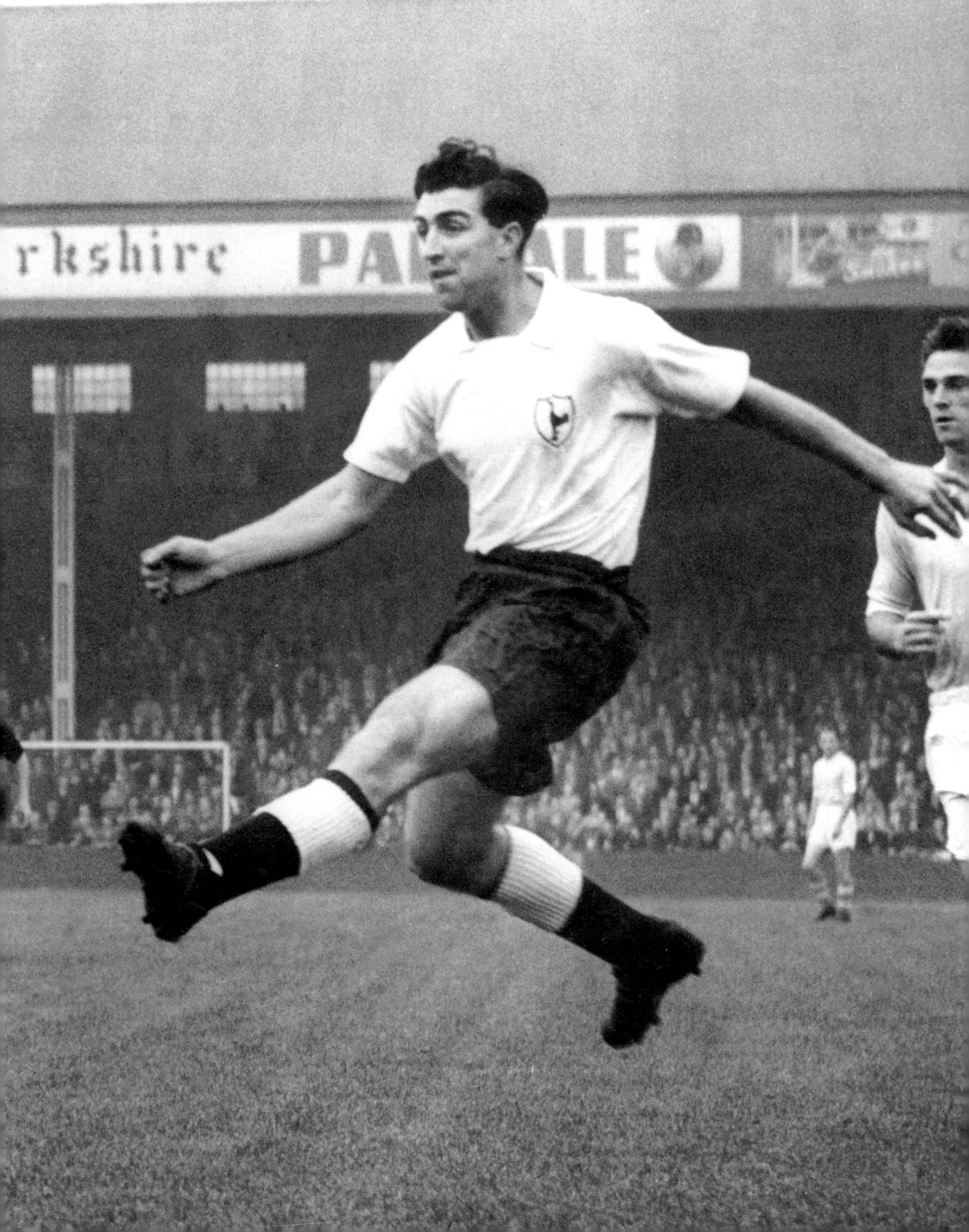
rkshire
PA
ALE

THE GAMES & THE GOALS

15.04.61 v Scotland at Wembley won 9-3

Bobby scored on 73 minutes to put England 5-2 up and then notched the last goal of the afternoon with five minutes remaining .

21.05.61 v Portugal at Lisbon drew 1-1

Bobby returned to the England line-up for this World Cup qualifier having missed the 8-0 drubbing of Mexico through injury.

14.04.62 v Scotland at Glasgow lost 0-2

Bobby's recalled after a five match absence.

27.02.63 v France at Paris lost 2-5

Bobby scored with a second half header after France had taken a 3-0 lead in a European Nations Cup tie second leg.

06.04.63 v Scotland at Wembley lost 1-2

Injured in a sixth minute collision, Bobby returned to the field just before half time.

08.05.63 v Brazil at Wembley drew 1-1 Friendly

29.05.63 v Czechoslovakia at Bratislava won 4-2

Bobby put England 2-0 up just before half time in this tour match.

02.06.63 v East Germany at Leipzig won 2-1 Tour match.

12.10.63 v Wales at Cardiff won 4-0

Jimmy Greaves supplied an outswinging centre which Bobby neatly headed into the net to open the scoring on five minutes. Midway through the second half Bobby shot England 3-0 ahead after another Greaves assist.

23.10.63 v Rest of the World at Wembley won 2-1

Bobby set up Terry Paine for England's opener in the game to mark the centenary of the Football Association.

20.11.63 v Northern Ireland at Wembley won 8-3

Bobby signed off the international scene with a goal just after half time to make the score 5-1.